Novels for Students, Volume 1

Copyright © 1997
Gale Research
835 Penobscot Building
645 Griswold St.
Detroit, Ml 48226-4094

This book is printed on acid-free paper that meets the minimum requirements of American National Standard for Information Sciences—Permanence Paper for Printed Library Materials, ANSI Z39.48-1984.

ISBN 0-7876-1686-9
ISSN 1094-3552

Printed in the United States of America
10 9 8 7 6 5

The Catcher in the Rye

J. D. Salinger

1951

Introduction

Although *The Catcher in the Rye* caused considerable controversy when it was first published in 1951, the book—the account of three disoriented days in the life of a troubled sixteen-year-old boy—was an instant hit. Within two weeks after its release, it was listed number one on *The New York Times* best-seller list, and it stayed there for thirty weeks. It remained immensely popular for many years, especially among teenagers and young adults, largely because of its fresh, brash style and anti-establishment attitudes—typical attributes of many people emerging from the physical and psychological turmoil of adolescence.

It also was the bane of many parents, who objected to the main character's obscene language, erratic behavior, and antisocial attitudes. Responding to the irate protests, numerous school and public libraries and bookstores removed the book from their shelves. Holden simply was not a good role model for the youth of the 1950s, in the view of many conservative adults. Said J. D. Salinger himself, in a rare published comment, "I'm aware that many of my friends will be saddened and shocked, or shock-saddened, over some of the chapters in *The Catcher in the Rye.* Some of my best friends are children. In fact, all my best friends are children. It's almost unbearable for me to realize that my book will be kept on a shelf out of their reach." The clamor over the book undoubtedly contributed to its popularity among the young: It became the forbidden fruit in the garden of literature.

For some reason—perhaps because of the swirling controversies over his written works—Salinger retreated from the New York literary scene in the 1960s to a bucolic New Hampshire community called Cornish, where he has lived a very private life and avidly avoided the press. Despite the fact that he has granted few interviews, there is a substantial body of critical and biographical works about Salinger and his all-too-brief list of literary creations.

Author Biography

Born in 1919 to a prosperous Manhattan family, Jerome David Salinger grew up in a New York City milieu not unlike that of young Holden Caulfield. Being a diligent student was never his first priority: After he flunked out of several prep schools, including the prestigious McBurney School, his parents sent him to Valley Forge Military Academy in Pennsylvania, from which he graduated in 1936. (Many people believe he modeled Pencey Prep, the fictional school attended by Caulfield, after Valley Forge.) He briefly attended Ursinus College, also in Pennsylvania, and New York University, where he stayed one month.

It was not until he took a short story course at Columbia University that Salinger officially launched his literary career. His teacher, Whit Burnett, was the founder and editor of *Story* magazine, which gave a headstart to a number of mid-century fiction writers. Salinger's first published piece appeared in *Story.* Then he moved rapidly into the big time of slick commercial magazines, writing short pieces for *Collier's, Saturday Evening Post, Esquire, Good Housekeeping, Cosmopolitan* and the upscale *New Yorker.*

Salinger has consistently refused to allow anyone to republish his early stories—those written between 1941 and 1948. (However, they may still lurk among the microfilm or microfiche copies of old magazines in local libraries.) Several are about draftees in World War II and may mirror Salinger's own military experiences in that war. He served in the Army Signal Corps and the Counter-Intelligence Corps from 1942 to 1945, participating in the Normandy campaign and the liberation of France. Winner of five battle stars, he still found a way to keep writing during this period, toting a portable typewriter around in the back of his Jeep (as did Holden's brother, D. B., in the novel).

The extant body of Salinger's work therefore consists (in addition to *The Catcher in the Rye*) of three collections of short stories: *Nine Stories* (1953), *Franny and Zooey* (1955) and *Raise High the Roof Beams* (1963)—plus, of course, his more recent book, *Hapworth 16, 1924* (1997), which is a republication of a former *New Yorker* novella.

Since the early 1960s, Salinger has lived in seclusion in rural New Hampshire, his privacy fiercely protected by loyal friends and neighbors. Married twice, he has two children, Margaret Ann and Matthew, from his second marriage. Both marriages ended in divorce.

Plot Summary

Part I—Holden Flunks out of Pencey Prep School

The Catcher in the Rye tells the story of Holden Caulfield, a teenage slacker who has perfected the art of underachievement. The novel begins with Holden flunking out of school for the fourth time. During the last days before his expulsion, he searches for an appropriate way to conclude his school experience, but he ends up getting so annoyed with his school and schoolmates that he leaves in the middle of the night on the next train home to New York City. Arriving home a few days earlier than his parents expect him, he hangs out in the city to delay the inevitable confrontation with his parents. When his money runs out, he considers hitchhiking out west, but he ultimately returns home, mainly to be with his younger sister Phoebe.

The first few chapters describe Holden's last days at Pencey Prep School in Agerstown, Pennsylvania. Advertisements portray Pencey as an elite school that grooms boys into sophisticated men, but Holden sees it as a nightmare of adolescence run amok. Fed up with everything about Pencey, Holden skips the football game against Pencey's rival to say good-bye to his history teacher, Mr. Spencer. He vaguely hopes that

Spencer might give him some comfort and useful advice, but Spencer is a sick old man who simply lectures him with a thousand platitudes about not applying himself. Like Spencer, the other teachers and administrators rarely spend any time mentoring boys because they are too busy spouting off platitudes or kissing up to the wealthy parents visiting the school.

Moreover, Pencey's students do not fit the prep school ideal any more than its teachers do. Holden's classmate Robert Ackley, for example, is the quintessential adolescent nerd. His acne and unbrushed teeth make him physically repulsive, while his annoying social habits—such as barging into the room uninvited, asking annoying questions, and refusing to leave when asked—make him a general nuisance. Other students, like Holden's roommate Ward Stradlater, initially appear sophisticated, but even they are really phonies. Stradlater seems good-looking, but he is secretly a slob who never cleans his rusty old razor. He also appears to be a successful student, but he is really an ungrateful egotist who gets other people to do his assignments. Nevertheless, Holden still feels a certain affection even for these annoying phonies. He is annoyed by Ackley but still invites him to the movies, and he sees through Stradlater's phoniness but also notices his occasional generosity.

The tension between Holden and his classmates eventually climaxes in a fight between Holden and Stradlater. Stradlater annoys Holden by asking him to write his English paper, so he can go on a date with Jane Gallagher, an old friend of Holden's. Stradlater really angers Holden, however, when he returns from the date and begins insinuating that he did all kinds of stuff with Jane in the back seat of a car. Fed up with Stradlater's phony nice-guy image, Holden picks a fight. Stradlater easily defeats the weaker Holden and gives him a bloody nose. After the fight, Holden retreats into Ackley's room to forget about Stradlater, but Ackley only makes Holden more lonely. Then Holden goes into the hall to escape Ackley, but the hall is just as lonely. Surrounded by Pencey's allpervasive loneliness, Holden decides to return home immediately instead of waiting for school to finish. He quickly packs and heads for the train station late at night, but before departing he vents his frustration with his schoolmates one last time. Yelling loud enough to wake everyone, he screams his final farewell to his moronic classmates.

Part II—Holden's Adventures in New York City

The middle section of the novel describes Holden's adventures in New York City. As soon as he arrives in New York, he looks for something to do, since it is too late to call his friends. He calls Faith Cavendish, a stripper recommended by a friend, but she does not want to meet a stranger so late. After a failed attempt to get a date with some girls in the hotel bar, he takes a cab to another bar in

Greenwich Village. When he returns to his hotel, a pimp named Maurice sets him up with a prostitute named Sunny, but Holden is too nervous to do anything with her. The next day Holden asks his old girlfriend, Sally Hayes, to a show. While waiting to meet her, he has breakfast with two nuns and buys a blues record for his sister. When he finally meets Sally, they go to a concert and go skating, but they eventually get into a fight and split up. After their fight, Holden meets an old classmate, Carl Luce, at the Wicker Bar, where they have a brief discussion until Holden gets drunk and starts asking inappropriately personal questions. After Carl leaves, the still-drunk Holden calls up Sally and makes a fool of himself.

Part III—Holden Returns Home

The last section of the novel describes Holden's return home. At first, Holden only wants to briefly say good-bye to his sister, Phoebe, so he sneaks into his house late at night in hopes of avoiding his parents. He successfully sneaks into the room where his sister sleeps, aided by the lucky coincidence that his parents are not home. At first, Phoebe is delighted to see Holden, but she gets upset when she realizes that he has flunked out again. She asks him why he flunked out, and he blames it on his terrible school. After listening to Holden's excuses, Phoebe criticizes him for being too pessimistic. Holden tries to deny this by explaining how he likes lots of things, but he can only think of a few: his dead brother Allie, a kid named James Castle who died at one of his schools, and Phoebe. In the end, Phoebe forces Holden to admit that he is a rather pessimistic failure. In the passage that gives the book its title, Holden explains that he cannot imagine himself fitting into any of the roles that society expects him to perform, like growing up to be a lawyer or scientist. Instead, he can only imagine being a catcher in the rye who stands at the edge of a large rye field watching over and protecting little kids from danger.

> "You know that song, 'If a body catch a body comin' through the rye'? I'd like—"

"It's 'If a body *meet* a body coming through the rye'!" old Phoebe said. "It's a poem. By Robert *Burns.*"

"I *know* it's a poem by Robert Burns."

She was right, though. It *is* "If a body meet a body coming through the rye." I didn't know it then, though.

"I thought it was 'If a body catch a body,'" I said. "Anyway, I keep picturing all these little kids playing some game in this big field of rye and all. Thousands of little kids, and nobody's around— nobody big, I mean—except me. And I'm standing on the edge of some crazy cliff. What I have to do, I have to catch everybody if they start to go over the cliff—I mean if they're running and they don't look where they're going I have to come out from somewhere and *catch* them. That's all I'd do all day. I'd be the catcher in the rye and all. I know it's crazy, but that's the only thing I'd really like to be. I know it's crazy."

In this passage, Salinger brilliantly blends the two sides of Holden's character. On the one hand, Holden admits that he *is* a failure: he is incapable of even imagining himself functioning in the adult world. On the other hand, however, Holden is not *only* a failure: he is also a deeply sensitive and compassionate person, albeit in an unorthodox way. In particular, he understands and cares about people who are outcasts or powerless. Phoebe seems to understand and accept this unorthodox sensitivity because she eventually reconciles herself to him, and they celebrate their reconciliation by dancing until their parents return and Holden has to sneak back out of the house.

After sneaking out of the house, Holden spends the night with his favorite teacher, Mr. Antolini, but he leaves early in the morning when he wakes up to find Mr. Antolini stroking his hair. Confused by such unusual behavior, Holden spends the morning wandering the streets until he eventually decides to hitchhike out west. He leaves a note at Phoebe's school telling her to meet him at the museum so they can say good-bye, but Phoebe shows up carrying her own belongings in a suitcase because she wants to go with Holden. At this point, Holden realizes how important they are to each other, and he finally decides to return home and face his parents. The novel never actually describes what happens next, but it suggests that Holden faces the dreadful confrontation with his parents and then later experiences some sort of nervous breakdown. The novel concludes with Holden looking back at all the people he has described and fondly remembering how he likes them despite their annoying and phony qualities.

Characters

Robert Ackley

Holden's unpleasant dormmate, whose personal habits are dirty and whose room stinks. Holden suspects that Ackley does not brush his teeth and describes them as mossy. Cursed with acne, Ackley constantly picks at the sores. Ackley dislikes Stadlater, calling him a "son of a bitch." Holden finds Ackley disgusting but appears to feel sorry for him at the same time.

Mr. Antolini

Holden's former English teacher, Mr. Antolini, "the best teacher I ever had," invited Holden to come right over, even though Holden probably woke him and his wife up in the middle of the night. Mr. Antolini asked why Holden was no longer at Pencey, warned him about heading for a fall, and wrote down a quote on paper for him: "The mark of the immature man is that he wants to die nobly for a cause, while the mark of the mature man is that he wants to live humbly for one." Later that night, after falling asleep on the couch, Holden wakes up to find Mr. Antolini patting his head in the dark. Holden leaps up, convinced Mr. Antolini is a pervert, and rushes out of the apartment. Later Holden is unsure whether his reaction was mistaken.

Allie Caulfield

Allie Caulfield is Holden's younger brother. While he has died of leukemia, he is very much alive throughout the book. Holden refers to him as still living and even talks to him. Bright and charming, Allie is/was Holden's best friend other than Phoebe.

D. B. Caulfield

D.B. Caulfield is Holden's and Phoebe's older brother. He is a successful and financially secure screenwriter in Hollywood. But Holden feels that D.B. has prostituted his art for money and should instead be writing serious works. While D.B. shows great solicitude for Holden, the relationship between the brothers is distant.

Holden Caulfield

Holden Caulfield is a deeply troubled sixteen-year-old boy who is totally alienated from his environment and from society as a whole. He looks on people and events with a distaste bordering on disgust. The reader can view him either as an adolescent struggling with the angst of growing up (the Peter Pan syndrome) or as a rebel against what he perceives as hypocrisy (phoniness) in the world of adults (i.e., society).

The novel is the recollection of three depressing days in Holden's life when his accumulated anger and frustration converge to create a life crisis. The events of this long weekend eventually propel him to a hospital where he is treated for both physical and mental disorders. Since the book is written in the first person, we see all people and events through Holden's eyes. He tells his story from the vantage point of the 17-year-old Caulfield, who is still in a California hospital at the outset of the book.

He begins with a statement of anger that includes the reader in its sarcasm:

> "If you really want to hear about it, the first thing you'll probably want to know is where I was born, and what my lousy childhood was like, and how my parents were occupied and all before they had me and all that David Copperfield kind of crap, but I don't feel like going into it, if you want to know the truth.… I'm not going to tell you my whole goddam autobiography or anything. I'll just tell you about this madman stuff that happened to me around last Christmas just before I got pretty run-down and had to come out here and take it easy.… Where I want to start telling about is the day I left Pencey Prep."

Holden has once again flunked out of prep school, where he failed every subject but English. On this day, he says goodbye to his history teacher, Mr. Spencer, who is home with the grippe. He views the sick man with both sympathy and disgust and escapes hastily after the teacher begins to lecture him about flunking out of three prep schools.

The novel continues with equally flawed encounters with two fellow students, Bob Ackley and his playboy roommate, Ward Stradlater. Holden decides to leave Pencey that very night.

He packs his belongings, heads to the railroad station and grabs a train to New York City. There he embarks on a harrowing weekend staying at hotels, frequenting bars, and trying desperately to communicate with everyone he meets—the mother of a classmate (to whom he lies about his identity), hangers-out in bars, taxi drivers, a prostitute and her pimp, and two nuns in a restaurant. His two most memorable encounters are with his old friend, the pseudo-sophisticated Sally Hayes, and a former schoolmate, Carl Luce. Both take place on Sunday.

Late Sunday night—thoroughly chilled from sitting in Central Park and having used up most of his money and everyone else's patience—Holden sneaks into his family's apartment. He wakes up his engaging ten-year-old sister, Phoebe. Phoebe is the only human being with whom Holden can communicate except for the memory of Allie, for whom he continually grieves. Phoebe represents the innocence and honesty of childhood, which is all Holden truly respects—a viewpoint shared in part by Salinger himself. (In contrast, Holden sees his older brother, D.B., as a "prostitute" because he has sold out his art, becoming a Hollywood scriptwriter instead of what Holden views as a serious writer.)

Phoebe is direct and blunt. When she learns that Holden has been expelled from yet another private school, her instant comment is, "Daddy'll *kill* you." And of course that's what Holden has been running away from all weekend—confronting his parents about his expulsion. Later, Phoebe tells him: "You don't like anything that's happening … You don't like any schools. You don't like a million things. You *don't.*" Holden is stunned and defensive. When he tries to think of something he likes, he finally comes down to nothing but Allie and Phoebe. He tells Phoebe that he's going to hitchhike to Colorado and start a new life there.

Still avoiding his parents, he arranges to spend the rest of Sunday night with a former favorite English teacher, Mr. Antolini, and his somewhat frowsy wife. During the night, he awakes to find Antolini stroking his hair. He immediately panics, deciding that Antolini is just another pervert in a world full of twisted people, and flees the Antolini apartment.

On Monday, he goes to Phoebe's school to leave a message for her to meet him at the Museum of Natural History. He wants to say goodbye. When Phoebe shows up, she is dragging a huge suitcase along the sidewalk. She intends to go with him. This is not in his plan at all. Instead, he takes her to the Central Park Zoo. While watching her ride on the merry-go-round, he worries that she'll fall off while trying to catch the gold ring. "The thing with kids is, if they want to grab for the gold ring, you have to let them do it, and not say anything. If they fall off, they fall off, but it's bad if you say anything to them," muses Caulfield. This, in a way, is the end of a dream he has told Phoebe:

> "... I keep picturing all these little kids playing some game in this big field of rye and all. Thousands of little kids, and nobody's around— nobody big, I mean—except me. And I'm standing on the edge of some crazy cliff. What I have to do, I have to catch everybody if they start to go over the cliff—I mean if they're running and they don't look where they're going. I have to come out from somewhere and *catch* them. That's all I'd do all day. I'd just be the catcher in the rye and all. I know it's crazy, but that's the only thing I'd really like to be. I know it's crazy."

Is this a turning point in Holden's withdrawal from the world—a point at which he know he has to accept the inevitable realities of life and people? Or will he continue to run away toward his dream of saving the world?

We leave Holden where we found him—or he found us—in the California hospital. When he is well, his brother D.B. will drive him back East, where he will attend yet another school.

Holden Caulfield is both tragic and funny, innocent and obscene, loving and cruel, clear-sighted yet viewing the world from a warped perspective, an expert in identifying phonies and the greatest phony himself. Of course, how you see Holden depends upon your own point of view. For many young readers of the book, especially in the 1950s and '60s, Holden still represented the true reality—the innocent abroad in a corrupt world. For older readers, he represents the angst of adolescence in its nightmarish extreme. For the ultraconservative, he still remains a threat to the status quo.

Phoebe Caulfield

Phoebe Caulfield, Holden Caulfield's pretty, redheaded ten-year-old sister, is straightforward and independent. She says exactly what she means. She does not share Holden's disenchanted view of the world. Quite the opposite, she scolds Holden for not liking anything at all. This hurts him very much because Phoebe is his favorite person—the only one with whom he can truly communicate. Phoebe is bright, well-organized, and creative. She keeps all her school work neatly in notebooks, each labeled with a different subject. She also loves to write books about a fictional girl detective named Hazle [sic] Weatherfield, but according to Holden, she never finishes them. Holden delights in taking her to the zoo and the movies and other places, as did their dead brother, Allie. Her directness and honesty are both refreshing and amusing.

Faith Cavendish

Faith Cavendish is the first person Holden calls when he gets to New York City. He met her previously at a party, where she was the date of a Princeton student. A burlesque stripper, she is supposed to be an "easy" conquest. She turns down Holden's invitation to get together and wishes him a nice weekend in New York.

Jane Gallagher

While she does not appear in the book, Jane Gallagher is very much present. Holden has a crush on this attractive and interesting young woman, who dances well and plays golf abominably. He resents the fact that his roommate, Stadlater, takes her out on a date and suspects that Stadlater, who likes to brag about his alleged sexual conquests, has forced her to have sex with him. When he first arrives in New York, Holden wants to call her up, but he never actually does so.

Sally Hayes

Sally Hayes is Holden's very attractive ex-girlfriend. He considers her stupid, possibly because she has an affected, pseudo-sophisticated manner. But he makes a date with her anyway. They go ice skating in Rockefeller Center, then go to a bar. Holden asks her to go away with him to Massachusetts or Vermont. She refuses, pointing out that they are much too young to set up housekeeping together and that college and Holden's career come first.

Holden doesn't want to hear about a traditional career. He becomes angry and tells Sally she's a "royal pain in the ass." She "hit the ceiling" and left. Later, drunk, he calls her late at night to tell her that, yes, he will come to help trim her family's Christmas tree.

Horwitz

Horwitz is the second taxi driver Holden encounters in New York City. Holden tries to strike up a conversation with him about where the ducks in Central Park go when the water in the lake freezes over. But Horwitz obviously considers Holden somewhat of a loony and is abrupt with him.

Carl Luce

Carl Luce, Holden's former schoolmate, ostensibly his Student Adviser, was about three years older and "one of these very intellectual guys —he had the highest I.Q. of any boy at Whooton."

Holden called him, hoping to have dinner and "a slightly intellectual conversation," but Luce could only meet him for a drink at the Wicker Bar at ten that evening.

He arrived saying he could only stay a few minutes, ordered a martini, kept trying to get Holden to lower his voice and change the subject.

Before leaving, he suggested that Holden call his father, a psychoanalyst, for an appointment.

Mrs. Morrow

Mrs. Morrow is the mother of Holden's classmate, Ernest. Holden runs into her on the train to New York. They have a superficial conversation in which Mrs. Morrow is very friendly. So is Holden—but he lies about his identity because he doesn't want Mrs. Morrow to know he has been kicked out of school.

Piano Player in the Wicker Bar

Holden encounters the Wicker Bar's "flitty" piano player in the men's room. He asks him to find out whether the waiter delivered his message to the singer, Valencia, whom Holden wanted to invite to his table. The piano man, seeing how drunk Holden is, tells him to go home.

Lillian Simmons

Lillian Simmons is D.B.'s ex-girlfriend. Holden's main observation about her: "She has big knockers." Holden encounters her in Ernie's, a Greenwich Village hangout, where she introduces Holden to her companion, Navy Commander "Blop."

Mr. Spencer

Mr. Spencer is Holden Caulfield's history teacher at Pencey. Before leaving on Saturday of his long weekend, Holden goes to Spencer's house to say goodbye. Spencer, ill with the grippe, is wearing pajamas and a bathrobe. Holden finds old men dressed this way to be pathetic, with their pale, skinny legs sticking out under their bathrobes and their pajama tops askew, revealing their pale, wispy chests. Spencer obviously likes Caulfield, but he cannot resist giving him a lecture on his poor performance in history. Holden listens, agrees, and leaves as soon as he can.

Ward Stradlater

Ward Stradlater is Holden's obnoxious roommate at Pencey Prep. A playboy, he asks Holden to write an essay on a room or a house for him while he goes out on a date with Jane Gallagher, the girl Holden really cares about. A resentful Holden writes an essay about his brother Allie's baseball glove, on which Allie scribbled Emily Dickinson poems. A secret slob (he shaves with a dirty, rusty razor), Stradlater makes a good appearance. Smooth and slick, he likes to boast about his alleged sexual prowess. When he returns from his date, he is irate because Holden has written an essay about a baseball glove instead of a house. Holden tears it up, has an argument with Stradlater, and ends up in a fistfight with him.

Sunny

Sunny is the prostitute Holden requests. When she comes to his room in the Edmont Hotel, she discovers that Holden just wants someone to talk with. She leaves in disgust. Later, she returns with her pimp, Maurice, the hotel's elevator operator. They demand another five dollars for her time. Holden protests, and after she takes the money from his wallet.

Three girls from Seattle

After checking ip and calling Faith Cavendish, Holden goes to the bar of the Edmont Hotel—"a goddam hotel" that was "full of perverts and morons," comments Holden. In the bar, he strikes up a conversation with three thirty-ish girls from Seattle who are spending their vacation touring New York City. He dances with them all, one by one, but the whole experience fizzles and he leaves the bar, calls a cab, and goes to Ernie's, a night club in Greenwich Village.

Two Nuns

Two nuns with whom Holden strikes up a conversation in a restaurant. They are both school teachers, and Holden charms them with his expressions of enthusiasm about English literature. Since they have a wicker collection basket with them, Holden gives them $10 as a contribution to their charity.

Themes

Alienation and Loneliness

The main theme that runs through this book is alienation, whether the book is read as the funny/tragic account of a deeply troubled, rebellious, and defensive teenager or as a commentary on a smug and meaningless social milieu. Phoebe sums up Holden's sense of separateness from and anger at other people when she tells him he doesn't like anything. Holden's red hunting cap, which he dons when he is most insecure, is a continuing symbol throughout the book of his feeling that he is different, doesn't fit into his environment, and, what's more, doesn't want to fit in.

Failure

A second theme is that of failure. Holden continually sets himself up for failure, then wears it like a badge of courage. Thus he fails in every encounter with other people in the book with the exception of Phoebe. Why would a sixteen-year-old want to fail? Failure serves as a great attention-getting device. And perhaps, more than anything, Holden wants attention from his parents, the absent characters in the book. What Holden really longs for, most likely, is acceptance and love.

Guilt and Innocence

Holden is deceitful and manipulative in most of his dealings with others. And he knows this all too well and even boasts of his prowess as a liar. But throughout the book we glimpse another Holden, the one who feels sorry for the people he cons. His basic kindness comes through in glimpses, particularly in the passage where he reveals that the only thing he would like to be is a "catcher in the rye" protecting innocent children from falling into the abyss of adulthood.

Anger

Holden is angry at everyone except Allie and Phoebe and perhaps the ducks in the pond in Central Park. Anger, of course, is the flip side of hurt. Holden is wounded by his disappointment in the faults of the world and frustrated because he finally realizes that he can't fix them. His failures may also be a way of acting out his anger at his parents and society at large.

Sexuality

Holden struggles with his emerging sexuality. He is unable to relate in any meaningful way to the girls he encounters along the way, writing them off as sex objects. He writes off other males as perverts or morons and views their sexuality with disgust. Confusion about sexual identity is common in adolescents. For Holden, it is terrifying.

Courage

Courage is one of the subtle themes running throughout the novel. Holden, in his own twisted way, confronts the demons in his life and, therefore, stands a chance of wrestling them to the floor.

Style

Narrator

In essence, we have three narrators of the events that take place in this book. The first is the author, J. D. Salinger, who was looking back in anger (or in creativity) from his thirty-two-year-old vantage point. The second is the seventeen-year-old Holden, still institutionalized, who tells the story as a recollection. And the third, and most immediate, is the sixteen-year-old Holden who does all the talking. The form of the narration is first person, in which a character uses "I" to relate events from his or her perspective.

Stream of Consciousness

The technique of the narration is a form known as "stream of consciousness." While the book proceeds in a rough chronological order, the events are related to the reader as Holden thinks of them. Wherever his mind wanders, the reader follows. Notice how his language often appears to be more like that of a ten-year-old than that of a smart sixteen-year-old. This is a continuing demonstration of Holden's unwillingness to grow up and join the hypocritical adult world that he despises. Holden's conversation in the Wicker Bar with Luce demonstrates this reluctance aptly, when Luce expresses annoyance at Holden's immaturity.

Setting

The settings for *The Catcher in the Rye*—Pencey Prep and New York City—were the settings for J. D. Salinger's early life as well, although the novel is not strictly autobiographical. Through his description of Holden's history teacher, Mr. Spencer, and his portrayals of Holden's fellow students, Salinger recreates the stifling atmosphere of a 1940s prep school, where a sense of alienation often resutled from not conforming to narrow social standards. The New York City where Holden spent his nightmare weekend is the same Manhattan where Salinger grew up—smaller, a little homier, and a lot less glitzy than the New York City of today. And Holden's home and family are similar to those of Salinger. However, Salinger had only one sibling, a brother. From the taxi ride, to the seedy hotel where Holden stayed, to Rockefeller Center to Central Park, Holden's New York is tangible, real, and plays an active role like any other character in the book. The descriptions of places and events are colorful and immediate. Salinger entices us into Holden's world whole and without resistance. He is a master of vivid story telling.

Symbolism

The book is rich in symbolism. The author drops hints of the meaning of its title twice before we find out what it is. The first time, Holden hears a little boy in New York sing-songing "If a body meet a body comin' through the rye," an Americanization of Robert Burns's poem and the song it inspired. The second time, Holden is with Phoebe and brings up the topic, referring to the song as "If a body *catch* a body comin' through the rye." Phoebe corrects him. But Holden's dream of being a catcher in the rye (derived from the second line of the poem) persists. He will save the children from adulthood and disillusionment.

Holden's red hat is an abiding symbol throughout the book of his self-conscious isolation from other people. He dons it whenever he is insecure. It almost becomes his alter ego. After he gives it to Phoebe, she gives it back to him. We do not know at the end of the book whether he still needs this equivalent of a security blanket.

Topics for Further Study

- Investigate current research on adolescent psychology. According to current theory, argue whether

Holden Caulfield is a typical troubled adolescent or a seriously mentally ill young man.

- Is Holden Caulfield a reliable narrator? Why or why not?

- Compare Holden's generation of the 1940s to today's generation. How are the two cultures similar and different?

Postwar Prosperity

The events in *The Catcher in the Rye* take place in 1946, only a year after the end of World War II. Adults at this time had survived the Great Depression and the multiple horrors of the war. Paradoxically, the war that wounded and killed so many people was the same instrument that launched the nation into an era of seemingly unbounded prosperity. During the postwar years, the gross national product rose to $500 billion, compared with $200 billion in prewar 1940. In unprecedented numbers, people bought houses, television sets, second cars, washing machines, and other consumer goods. No wonder the nation wanted to forget the past and to celebrate its new beginnings. The celebration took the form of a new materialism and extreme conservatism. Traditional values were the norm. People did not want to hear from the Holden Caulfields and J. D. Salingers of the era. They were in a state of blissful denial.

Holden has withdrawn from this society enough to see it from a different perspective. He abhors the banality and hypocrisy he sees in the adult world and is therefore reluctant to participate in it, so his behavior, while that of an adolescent trying to affirm his own identity, also symbolizes the perceived shallowness of people and society.

Most of the things Holden fears peak in the 1950s, when conservatism, rigid morality, and paranoid self-righteousness held the nation in a tight grip. Small wonder that 1950s parents assailed Salinger's novel when it hit book stores and libraries in 1951. It undermined the foundations of their beliefs and threatened to unsettle their placid but pleasant existence, which was sustained by their hatred of an outside enemy—communism.

Cold War Concern

Despite the materialistic prosperity of the 1950s, many people were concerned about what appeared to be a troubling future. The Soviet Union acquired nuclear technology soon after the war, and the successful launch of the first artificial satellite, Sputnik, in 1957 appeared to give the Russians a threatening advantage over the United States. Americans also questioned the success of their educational system, which had failed them in the space race. The fear of nuclear war became so pervasive that students were regularly drilled on how to "duck and cover" in the case of an attack, and many families built bomb shelters in their backyards and stocked them with food and other supplies to survive a possible holocaust.

Education

In 1950 about ten percent of all children were educated in Catholic schools, which at the time received federal funding. This became a topic for debate as people disputed whether or not private institutions should receive taxpayer money. Public schools that employed Roman Catholic nuns as teachers also became a target of debate, as some states, such as Wisconsin, denied these schools public support. Such actions were supported by the National Education Association, which took a strong antireligious stance. On the other hand, the National Catholic Educational Association argued that Catholic citizens supported public schools, and so it was unfair to deny parochial schools funding when they were meeting the same educational goals. Religion was more prevalent in public schools during the 1950s; religious topics were routinely taught in public schools: students listened to Bible readings (which were required in twelve states and the District of Columbia), and many students were given "released-time" breaks, during which they were allowed to leave school for one hour a week to attend religious classes.

Pressure to Conform

Social pressures to conform were intense in the 1950s, not only in politics but also within the nation's educational system, which enjoyed multiple infusions of government funds. A college education became the passport to prosperity, especially after the G.I. bill of 1944 helped pay for war veterans' higher education. Corporations grew rapidly to meet the increasing demands of consumers and sopped up the growing number of skilled employees. Dress codes and embedded company cultures muted individualism. Jobs for white males were secure, while women stayed home and raised the many children ushered in by the postwar "Baby Boom."

The Growing Generation Gap

The "Baby Boom" caused Americans to pay more attention to the younger generation. While *Catcher in the Rye* was somewhat before its time in this regard, the subject had particular relevance in the years after its publication. Lifestyles began to change dramatically as teenagers began to date and become sexually active at a younger age. Teenagers became more rebellious, a trend that their parents viewed to be strongly influenced by a new, decadent form of music called rock 'n' roll. This new attitude of rebelliousness was typified by Hollywood actors such as James Dean and Marlon Brando, the bohemian lifestyle of the beatniks, and later in the literature of Jack Kerouac and Alan Ginsberg. Juvenile delinquency became an alarming problem and was considered a major social issue. Teens were skipping classes and committing crimes, and parents were alarmed by their children's lack of respect for authority.

Compare & Contrast

- **1950s:** Religion is an integral part of many classrooms. Bible readings and regular lessons about religious topics are included in course plans.

Today: The separation of Church and State is rigorously upheld and children do not study religious texts; prayer in schools becomes a burning issue, and there is growing pressure from religious factions to have educators teach creationism to counterbalance lessons in Charles Darwin's theory of evolution.

- **1950s:** Only about 58% of students finish high school, but jobs are so plentiful that employment rates remain high. Employer loyalty is the norm, and employees often remain with one company until they retire.

Today: Most employers that offer jobs with living-wage incomes require employees to have college degrees, even for low-level positions. Routine layoffs and downsizing largely eliminate company loyalty, and it becomes common for workers to switch jobs and even careers.

- **1950s:** Classroom curricula focus on basic skills, including reading, writing, and arithmetic, but the inclusion of science in classes becomes a growing priority as the educational system tries to prepare students for the needs of a more technology-oriented world.

Today: Educators aim to give students wellrounded educations that include sex education and an emphasis on multicultural studies; parents become concerned that children are not being taught the basics and that high school students are graduating without knowing how to read. Educators recognize the need to train students in the use of computers, which become common equipment in classrooms and libraries.

- **1950s:** Postwar prosperity brings with it a preoccupation with material goods as the middleclasses enjoy unprecedented buying power; children begin to rebel against this crass materialism and conservatism, and nonconformist icons like actor James Dean become popular.

Today: Adults who were the rebellious children of the 1950s and 1960s long for a return of the "family values" of the 1950s; "family values" becomes a campaign buzz phrase for politicians as the American people return to conservative beliefs.

Critical Overview

Mixed reviews greeted J. D. Salinger's first novel, *The Catcher in the Rye*, published on July 16, 1951. *New York Times* critic Nash K. Burger, for example, lauded the book as "an unusually brilliant first novel," and *Chicago Tribune* reviewer Paul Engle called the novel "engaging and believable." In contrast, T. Morris Longstreth stated in the *Christian Science Monitor* that "the book was not fit for children to read." Regarding Holden Caulfield, the book's teenage narrator and protagonist, Longstreth wrote: "Fortunately there cannot be many of him yet. But one fears that a book like this given wide circulation may multiply his kind—as too easily happens when immorality and perversion are recounted by writers of talent whose work is countenanced in the name of art of good intention." In the novel's defense, critic James Bryan wrote in *PMLA:* "The richness of spirit in this novel, especially of the vision, the compassion and the humor of the narrator, reveal a psyche far healthier than that of the boy who endured the events of this narrative. Through the telling of his story, Holden has given shape to, and thus achieved control of, his troubled past."

It can be argued that *The Catcher in the Rye* is as much a critique of society as a revelation of the rebellion and angst of a teenage boy. The book takes potshots at a post-World War II society full of self-righteousness and preoccupied by the pursuit of the "American Dream" of everlasting prosperity. Salinger depicts this goal as being empty and meaningless. Commented the great American novelist William Faulkner, who praised Salinger's novel, "When Holden attempted to enter the human race, there was no human race there."

The reader never finds out how Holden turns out. Will he compromise with the realities of people and society, becoming like the people he despised? Will the banality of everyday events engulf his reluctant coming of age, leaving him a tormented misfit for the rest of his life? Or will he become a superhero, leading others out of the slough of the ordinary and into a more enlightened view of life? The reader will never know unless Salinger writes a sequel. His most recent novel, *Hapworth 16, 1924*, released in the spring of 1997, is a republication of a long short story that appeared in the *New Yorker* in the 1960s. The featured character in the new book is Seymour Glass, member of another well-to-do fictional New York family depicted in a number of Salinger short stories. For some readers and critics, however, the endless saga of the eccentric Glass family eventually wore out its welcome. *The Catcher in the Rye* and *Hapworth 16, 1924* are the only two novels Salinger has thus far written. But he did write a wealth of short stories for such magazines as the *New Yorker, Saturday Evening Post*, and *Collier's*.

If *The Catcher in the Rye* were introduced as a new book today, it would certainly not be considered as shocking now as it was in the 1950s.

But it would still be viewed as a true and vivid portrait of adolescent angst. It can therefore rightly take its place among the literary classics of the twentieth century.

Sources

James Bryan, "The Psychological Structure of *The Catcher in the Rye,*" *PMLA: Publications of the Modern Language Association*, Vol. 89, no. 5, 1974, pp. 1065-74.

Nash K. Burger, "Books of *The Times,*" in *New York Times*, July 16, 1951, p. 19.

Paul Engle, "Honest Tale of Distraught Adolescent," in *Chicago Sunday Tribune Magazine of Books*, July 15, 1951, p. 3.

William Faulkner, "A Word to Young Writers," in *Faulkner in the University: Class Conferences at the University of Virginia 1957-1958*, edited by Frederick L. Gwynn and Joseph L. Blotner, University of Virginia Press, 1959, pp. 244-45.

T. Morris Longstreth, "New Novels in the News," in *Christian Science Monitor*, July 19, 1951, p. 11.

For Further Study

Jonathan Baumbach, "The Saint as a Young Man: A Reappraisal of *The Catcher in the Rye,*" in *Modern Language Quarterly*, Vol. 25, no. 4, December, 1964, pp. 461-72.

> This defense of *The Catcher in the Rye* valorizes Holden's childlike innocence as a form of saintly idealism.

Harold Bloom, "Introduction," in *Major Literary Characters*, edited by Harold Bloom, Chelsea House, 1996, pp. 1-4.

> A general analysis of the character Holden Caulfield which situates him relative to other literary figures.

Donald P. Costello, "The Language of *The Catcher in the Rye,*" in *American Speech*, Vol. 34, no. 3, October, 1959, pp. 172-81.

> An analysis of how Salinger's use of language realistically portrays American teenage slang during the 1950s.

Duane Edwards, "Holden Caulfield: Don't Ever Tell Anybody Anything," in *English Literary History*, Vol. 44, no. 3, Fall, 1977, pp. 556-67.

> This analysis of the character of Holden Caulfield emphasizes how

Holden is an ironic character who exemplifies the same kind of phoniness that he criticizes in others.

Warren French, *J. D. Salinger, Revisited*, Twayne Publishers, 1988.

This book provides an overview of Salinger's life and fiction, and one of its chapters also contains an excellent introduction to the themes and issues raised in *The Catcher in the Rye*.

Lilian Furst, "Dostoyevsky's *Notes from Underground* and Salinger's *The Catcher in the Rye*," in *Canadian Review of Comparative Literature*, Vol. 5, no. I, Winter, 1978, pp. 72-85.

An analysis of parallels between *The Catcher in the Rye* and Dostoyevsky's *Notes from Underground*

Arthur Heiserman and James E. Miller, Jr., "J. D. Salinger: Some Crazy Cliff," in *Western Humanities Review*, Vol. 10, no. 2, Spring, 1956, pp. 129-37.

An analysis of *The Catcher in the Rye* which shows how it belongs to the western literary tradition of epic quest narratives.

John M. Howell, "Salinger in the Waste Land," in *Critical Essays on J. D. Salinger's* The Catcher in the Rye, edited by Joel Salzberg, G. K. Hall & Co., 1990, pp. 85-91.

An analysis of parallels between *The*

Catcher in the Rye and T. S. Eliot's poetry.

Charles Kaplan, "Holden and Huck: The Odysseys of Youth," in *College English*, Vol. 18, no. 2, November, 1956, pp. 76-80.

> A comparison of *The Catcher in the Rye* to Mark Twain's *Huckleberry Finn.*

Robert A. Lee, "'Flunking Everything Else Except English Anyway': Holden Caulfield, Author," in *Critical Essays on J. D. Salinger's* The Catcher in the Rye, edited by Joel Salzberg, G. K. Hall, 1990, pp. 185-97.

> An analysis of Holden's character which focuses on his artistic creativity.

Carol and Richard Ohmann, "Reviewers, Critics, and *The Catcher in the Rye,"* in *Critical Inquiry*, Vol. 3, no. 1, Autumn, 1976, pp. 15-37.

> A Marxist analysis of how capitalist social and economic strategies influence the development of Holden's character.

Jack Salzman, "Introduction," in *New Essays on* The Catcher in the Rye, edited by Jack Salzman, Cambridge University Press, 1991, pp. 1-22.

> An overview of critical interpretations of *The Catcher in the Rye.*

Mary Suzanne Schriber, "Holden Caulfield, C'est Moi," in *Critical Essays on J. D. Salinger's* The Catcher in the Rye, edited by Joel Salzberg, G. K. Hall, 1990, pp. 226-38.

> A feminist analysis of the critical reception of *The Catcher in the Rye* which argues that male critics inflate the significance of the novel because they identify with Holden as a representation of their own male adolescence and because they ignore female perspectives.

Helen Weinberg,*The New Novel in America: The Kafkan Mode in Contemporary Fiction*, Cornell University Press, 1970.

> An analysis of parallels between The *Catcher in the Rye* and Franz Kafka's fiction.

Lightning Source UK Ltd.
Milton Keynes UK
UKHW020740300123
416172UK00014B/637

9 781375 398015